Original title:
The Roof That Protects Me

Copyright © 2025 Creative Arts Management OÜ
All rights reserved.

Author: Ophelia Ravenscroft
ISBN HARDBACK: 978-1-80587-223-8
ISBN PAPERBACK: 978-1-80587-693-9

Fortress of Solace

In my little fortress, I sip my tea,
The cat looks regal, all judging me.
While I wear pajamas that are two sizes too wide,
She rules the kingdom, tail high with pride.

The fridge is my treasure, the couch my throne,
With chips in a bowl, I'm never alone.
A fortress of snacks and Netflix galore,
Who needs a castle? I've got the floor.

Nestled in Serenity

In a nest of blankets, I curl up tight,
My remote's my scepter in the long, long night.
The dog snorts and snores as I scroll away,
Dreaming of days where I could save the day.

Yet here I stay, with my loyal pup,
A king on his pillow, both cozy and sup.
With popcorn in hand and a smile wide,
This serene little kingdom fills me with pride.

The Upper Embrace

Up here on my perch, I watch the world sway,
With birds that sing off-key and kids at play.
I'm snuggled in cushions that bear the weight,
Of dreams of adventure, but hey, it's late!

A fortress of laughter, my ceiling is low,
While outside are heroes, dressed up for the show.
But I know my cape is a robe with a hood,
And my snack stash is better than fighting for good.

Tapestry of Tranquility

Life spins a tapestry, I thread my own way,
With yarns of mischief that brighten my day.
The pets hold a meeting in the warm afternoon,
Plotting to steal snacks with utmost cartoon.

So I craft my adventure in quilted delight,
With laughter and chaos that feels just right.
For every soft stitch in this life that I weave,
Makes home in my heart, where I never leave.

Guardian of Warmth

When rain drops dance on my head,
I stay snug, tucked up in bed.
Fluffy socks on my chilly feet,
While outside, a flood's on repeat.

The sky might frown, the clouds may weep,
Yet here I laugh, and drift to sleep.
My cereal sings a crunching tune,
As squirrels argue over a moon.

A cat on my lap claims her throne,
With purrs that warm me like a phone.
In a fort of cushions, I'll reside,
With snacks and Netflix by my side.

So let it storm, let winds jest,
Inside my haven, I'm truly blessed.

Embrace of Solitude

In a fortress built of pillows high,
Privacy thick as a sweet pie.
I wear my blanket like a cape,
A solo superhero with no cape.

The clock ticks loud like a comedic beat,
Tickle my thoughts with its off-tune greet.
I pour some tea that leaves me bemused,
While socks in mismatches are proudly fused.

The fridge hums in a whimsical tune,
As I dance with the broom to a silly cartoon.
Unseen by the world, I craft my dream,
The universe waiting for my grand scheme.

All alone, but never quite lonely,
Stirring up laughter, rather homely.

Silent Watcher Above

Up in the sky, the sun grins wide,
While shadows shape a comical slide.
Clouds lounge around like they own the place,
Unaware they're just covering space.

First it's a bunny, then a big car,
Imagination flies as high as a star.
I share secrets with the birds in flight,
Who tweet back with laughter that's pure delight.

The moon winks at me, a goofy guide,
Or maybe it's just pranking the tide.
With midnight snacks, we share a feast,
As the cat will jump me; it's quite a beast.

In this watchtower, I find my glee,
As the world below is too wild for me.

The Arch of Assurance

Arching above with a comedic flair,
Shields me from troubles and all kinds of care.
Raindrops tap in a ticklish way,
While I cozy up to a bright array.

With colors that cheer, a gradient ride,
It's my jester's cap, with joy as my guide.
Twinkling lights race across the lane,
Making silly shadows dance in the rain.

Weather forecasts may shout and rant,
But here I'm safe with my dancing plant.
Each flick of a leaf brings a chuckle or two,
As I sip my cocoa, I'm starting anew.

So let the storms and gusts all play,
Under this arch, I'll laugh all day.

Stay Dry, Stay Dreaming

When raindrops fall like little clowns,
I dance inside while thunder frowns.
With every drip, a new dream springs,
I'm safe from all the storm's wild flings.

The puddles splash in giddy glee,
As I sip tea, oh can't you see?
This cozy spot, my happy zone,
Where laughter echoes, never alone.

Shield Against the Storm

The wind may howl, the skies may grump,
But here I am, not feeling stumped.
With sips of soup, I hold my ground,
A fortress built from giggles found.

Under my shield, no worries climb,
I wear my cheer like a quirky rhyme.
The storm could rage for all it cares,
I'll jump and laugh, despite the flares.

Embrace of the Timbers

These wooden beams, my pals so dear,
They keep away my doubt and fear.
With every creak, a silly joke,
We giggle up while tempest chokes.

The rafters hum a merry tune,
While rain performs a soggy swoon.
We share our secrets, dreams of flight,
Together here, we shine so bright.

A Canopy of Comfort

Beneath this top of dreams and play,
I snuggle close as skies turn gray.
With cozy socks and silly hats,
I lounge around, avoiding spats.

The raindrops dance a funny jig,
They tap a rhythm, oh so big.
I'll kick and spin in my safe space,
In this snug patch, I find my grace.

Cradle of Dreams

Beneath this not-so-sturdy spread,
My circus of thoughts often dances ahead.
In socks mismatched, I make my stand,
With pillows as shields, I'll fight the bland.

The cat thinks it's a throne of grace,
While I tumble in, an upside-down face.
Every creak's a ghost, every squeak's a tale,
In this cozy chaos, I shan't fail.

The ceiling is painted with dreams so wide,
Of flying to space on a purple slide.
I giggle and wiggle, what a delight,
In this bouncy castle, my dreams take flight.

So here I will stay, a jester at play,
With crumbs of adventure strewn in my way.
A fortress of laughter, a haven of glee,
Where giggles echo, and I'm utterly free.

Protectress of the Night

When evening twirls in her velvet cape,
I pull up my covers and escape.
With shadows lurking, it's quite a sight,
But I've got my buddy—a nightlight bright.

It guards against nightmares, almost like magic,
Although sometimes it flickers, which is quite tragic.
I laugh at the critters that seem to creep,
They're probably just trying to join in my sleep.

The moon beams in like a snoozing owl,
Whispering secrets with a soft, wise scowl.
We share our giggles in the moon's embrace,
As I dream of donuts, oh, what a place!

My fortress of giggles, my bubble of cheer,
Where monsters are friends, and there's nothing to fear.
So close your eyes, let the nonsense flow,
In the night's comedy, let your laughter glow!

Fortification of the Heart

In a fortress built with candy hearts,
Laughter echoes and joyous arts.
With marshmallow walls and licorice towers,
I reign like a king in sweet, silly hours.

Though chocolate storms may come my way,
I'll dance in the rain, giggling all day.
For every hiccup, there's giggle-gold,
A treasure of laughter that never grows old.

Here's where I'm safe with a splash of sass,
Where jokes and jests can build up en masse.
My heart's a castle, my smile a gate,
Inviting all jesters to celebrate fate.

So let's throw a party, let merriment start,
In this land of whimsy, oh, what a chart!
With jesters and jesting, the fun is a spark,
In this fortress of love, we'll dance till it's dark!

A Wave of Security

Riding the waves of giggles and glee,
I float on a raft made of jellybeans, see?
With gummy sharks and sweet fish that sing,
I proudly pretend to be the jelly king.

The tides may be wild, but I hold on tight,
With arms wide open, I thrill in the flight.
I splash in the puddles of joy and of cheer,
In this ocean of laughter, I've nothing to fear.

When the clouds start to grumble, I twirl and I spin,
For laughter's the anchor that pulls me back in.
With sunshine and rainbows, I dance on my waves,
Creating a symphony that giggle-graves.

So join me, my friend, on this surf of delight,
With tides of amusement and dreams shining bright.
In this vast ocean where silliness flows,
I'll paddle my boat wherever it goes!

Embrace of the Overhead

When clouds parade in the sky,
I wonder if they're feeling shy.
Do they know they're my overhead?
Softly cushioning my silly head.

A bird could dive, a plane could glide,
As I munch on chips with pride.
Do they laugh at my shared snack?
"Take a bite!" they surely quack.

The sun beams down with goofy rays,
While I chase shadows in a daze.
Beneath this fluff, I strike a pose,
Waving to birds as they doze.

So here I sit, my heart afloat,
Dodging drops from the raincoat.
With giggles echoing all around,
In this canopy, joy is found.

The Shelter of Shadows

Underneath the leafy trees,
I find my thoughts drift in the breeze.
Squirrels chatter, they gossip loud,
Judging my snacks, oh, what a crowd!

A lizard sunbathes, strikes a pose,
While ants march in with tiny woes.
I laugh as they scurry and scold,
"What's your plan, little friend, so bold?"

The sun's like a spotlight on this stage,
As critters dance, acting their age.
I'm their audience, chuckling away,
In this shadowed splash of play.

Here in the wild, I'm always safe,
From weird bird songs, or leaping waif.
Wrapped in giggles, life's a blast,
In the shelter where joy contrasts.

Auras of Peace

In the morning, I spy the sky,
Where fluff and giggles fly high.
A soft breeze whispers silly tunes,
Serenading lazy afternoons.

The sun does a silly little jig,
While I munch on a carrot big.
"Be more orange!" the vegetables tease,
As I smile at their goofy pleas.

Butterflies flit, with colors bright,
Chasing dreams into the light.
I giggle as they chase my hat,
Confetti of smiles, imagine that!

In moments sweet, the world's a game,
Beneath this glow, it's all the same.
Wrapped in charm, I take my ease,
Under the auras, my heart is pleased.

Veil of Quietude

With curtains drawn, the light plays shy,
As I lounge here, oh me, oh my!
The cat sprawls out, taking the space,
Dreaming of worlds, with a silly face.

Whispers float like floating dots,
While I plot out some cooking pots.
"Chop chop!" says a mischievous spoon,
"Let's make soup by the light of the moon!"

This tranquil space is my own throne,
Where back and forth, I freely moan.
Each giggle bubbles, laughter streams,
Creating a melody of dreams.

In this soft nest, I daydream deep,
While shadows dance and secrets creep.
Enveloped in warmth, I close my eyes,
Behind this veil, fun never dies.

A Canopy for the Soul

Beneath the cover, squirrels dance,
Rain or shine, they take a chance.
A shaded place for picnic fare,
Watch out for ants that love to share.

Umbrellas up but drinks go down,
A canopy makes us laugh, not frown.
Birds chirp jokes, we roll with glee,
Under this shade, we're all so free.

Breezes tickle our sunny woes,
Hat lost to wind, oh how it blows!
Laughter echoes, we find our peace,
Together here, our joy won't cease.

With each giggle, the world's alright,
This covered ground is pure delight.
A colorful quilt in the sky,
Where smiles flourish and worries fly.

The Mantle of Bliss

A cloak of laughter wraps us tight,
Cracked umbrellas can bring delight.
Under this silly patchwork dome,
We laugh so hard, we call it home.

Dodging raindrops like playful foes,
Running in circles, away it goes.
Each trip, a giggle takes its flight,
Inside this shelter, the jokes feel bright.

A fortress made of whimsical dreams,
Covered in laughter, bursting at the seams.
Here we feast on cake and pie,
With mashed-up clouds, we reach the sky.

As thunder rolls and lightning plays,
We dance and chuckle in funny ways.
This mantle, our joyous parade,
In every storm, our fun won't fade.

Serenity in the Open Air

Under the branches, we lay and play,
Nature's blanket, come what may.
Crickets sing their evening tune,
While fireflies start a light the moon.

Kittens scamper, chasing their tails,
Picnic snacks beware of snails!
We laugh as sandwiches take flight,
The ants arrive, oh what a sight!

Each breeze a tickle, a playful jest,
Clouds float by, let's make a nest.
With belly laughs and bug spray in hand,
We create memories, oh so grand.

In this sanctuary, laughter's the key,
A haven of joy, just you and me.
With giggles echoing, no sign of despair,
Serenity lives in this open air.

Clouds of Support

Pillowy puffs hold up our cheer,
Who knew clouds could be so dear?
They catch our dreams in fluffy embrace,
As we tumble through this silly space.

Sunshine giggles, while rainbows grin,
Every drop tells a joke within.
"Why don't we float?" one thought deploys,
And clouds reply with raucous joys.

Umbrellas spin, it's quite the show,
As we twist and twirl to the clouds' flow.
Here's to mischief in every gust,
In funny weather, we place our trust.

Supportive sky, we dance and sway,
In laughter's arms, we choose to play.
Life's a comedy, let laughter ignite,
Under these clouds, everything feels right.

A Ceiling of Calm

Above me lies a ceiling wide,
A limit for my thoughts to glide.
When the world gets a little loud,
I can hide away, far from the crowd.

While rain might pour with all its might,
I giggle as drops try to take flight.
The roof above just softly grins,
As I escape from daily sins.

The ceiling hums a gentle tune,
While I craft plans for a grand balloon.
It sways a bit, but holds its ground,
In this fortress of fun, I am crowned.

So let the storms rage on outside,
Here I'll perch, I won't abide.
With a snack in hand and jokes to beam,
Life's a laugh under this ceiling dream.

Refuge Beneath the Stars

Underneath the sky so bright,
I pretend it's a canvas of pure light.
The stars above, they twinkle and wink,
As I plot my plans with a mischievous link.

I've built a blanket fort so high,
With crumpled snacks, and juice nearby.
The cosmos watches my every laugh,
As I sip on juice in my cozy raft.

Neighbors gawk at my peculiar ways,
But who needs prying in their gaze?
I'm a cosmic captain with dreams so bold,
Guided by constellations, stories untold.

Moonbeams chuckle as I take my seat,
Mapping out pals and snacks to meet.
Beneath this celestial delight I dwell,
In the laughter of nights where I thrive so well.

A Haven from the Elements

When wind decides to twist and shout,
I find my comfort, no room for doubt.
With walls so sturdy, I can't complain,
While outside gets soaked in the rain.

Alongside this haven, cozy and snug,
I sip on cocoa, give the mug a hug.
As thunder rolls like a metal band,
I dance to the rhythm with a spoon in hand.

The sun might blaze like a fiery beast,
But inside I'm lounging, enjoying the feast.
With ice cream melting, but spirits up high,
In this sanctuary, I float through the sky.

So let the weather do its thing,
With each storm breeze, my soul takes wing.
In a world of chaos, here I remain,
In my refuge from the elements, never mundane.

Shielding Dreams

In the attic where all my hopes reside,
This fortress of laughter, my playful guide.
A pillow fort bustling with giggles and cheer,
Where every shade of worry disappears.

As shadows creep, I make a scene,
Surrounded by plush, never too keen.
I wear my crown of crumpled dreams,
And plot silly schemes with marshmallow beams.

Against the world's crazy, I stand my ground,
With a shield of giggles, I'm glory-bound.
No worries here under this whimsical might,
Just sparkles of joy that dance in the night.

So let them knock, let the world outside clash,
I'm secure in my fortress, my silly stash.
With dreams afloat like balloons in the air,
In this shield of laughter, I've nothing to spare.

Sanctuary in the Sky

Up above where pigeons coo,
I hide from rain, oh what a view!
A quirky hat, my shield today,
With squirrels dancing, come what may.

The ceiling's peeling, oh what fun,
It's like a game, but I have won.
With every leak, a tale unfolds,
A circus act, brave, and bold!

Neighbors peek through windows bright,
I wave with glee, it's quite a sight.
A safety net made of old toys,
In my fortress of endless joys.

So here I sit, a king on high,
With jellybeans and donuts nigh.
In my odd little sky retreat,
Life's just a show with a fun beat!

Beneath a Blanket of Security

Under my quilt, I snuggle tight,
With snacks and giggles, feels just right.
Coffee spills on the fluff and fold,
But who cares when you're cozy and bold?

A fortress built with pillows high,
Each one a cloud, floating by.
The cat joins in, my soft brigade,
We're launching into a dream parade!

Loud thunder roars, but that's okay,
We'll dance till dawn, in our quirky way.
The blanket cape, it flutters wide,
Imagination takes us for a ride.

So here we dwell, in laughter's hold,
With tales of pirates and knights of old.
Each sip of cocoa, my shield, my friend,
In this joy-filled haven, may it never end!

The Dome of Comfort

Here under cover, safe from strife,
I juggle muffins, it's a sweet life.
The ceiling spins, in dizzying glee,
My laugh escapes, a wild decree!

Spot the odd sock, it tells a tale,
Of laundry battles, I cannot fail.
With snacks piled high, and friends around,
A dome of comfort, joy abounds.

A little wiggle, the dance begins,
In this fortress, we are all twins.
With every chuckle that fills the room,
We light the night with laughter's bloom.

From ceiling beams to floor below,
Each goofy moment makes my heart glow.
Within these walls, I'm never alone,
In my quirky castle, I've found my home!

Enclosed by Grace

Cushions piled like clouds so sweet,
My secret lair, a cozy seat.
With every giggle and silly face,
I've found pure joy in this silly space.

Ice cream drips, it paints the floor,
A masterpiece that I adore.
A safety net of laughter bright,
We dance with socks in silly flight.

The dog joins in, a furry friend,
He shakes his tail, I cannot pretend.
In this little nook, time slips away,
Each moment wrapped in fun and play.

So here I dwell, a whimsied grace,
Crafting memories in this sacred place.
With friends and treats, oh how I cheer,
In my bubble of bliss, I hold them near!

The Fortress of Familiar Faces

In a castle made of socks and shoes,
My dog holds court, so much to lose.
Random stickers on the wall,
Squeaky toys, my mind's freefall.

Lego bricks guard my every thought,
While raucous laughter fills the spot.
With every meal, a new surprise,
Burnt toast and pizza make me wise.

The fridge hums with its loyal tune,
The microwave dances—what a boon!
In this fortress, I reign supreme,
Familiar faces in my dream.

Who needs armor when you've got snacks?
My fortress rules—no need for hacks!
With a cat on guard, so sly and keen,
I'll conquer boredom, my royal scene.

Beneath My Comforting Cover

Underneath the fluff and seams,
I hide from chores and big kid dreams.
The blanket fort is my delight,
With pillows piled and nap-time right.

Sneezes echo from beneath the drape,
As I concoct a master shape.
A fortress made of snack attack,
With chocolate bars all in my pack.

Silly cartoons play on loop,
While I embrace my happy troop.
Adventure waits behind my shield,
In this world, I never yield.

So pass the chips and guard the fun,
With every giggle, we've already won!
Gnawing joy, like a silly song,
Here's where I know I truly belong.

Shelter from the Storm

In sideways rain, I dash inside,
Where comfort blooms and fears subside.
With socks that clash and hopes that swell,
This quirky den fits me so well.

A chicken hat upon my head,
Popcorn kernels in my bed.
The storm can't reach this cozy nook,
As I dive into my latest book.

Dancing spoons and forks on the floor,
Join the party—what a score!
While thunder rumbles like a joke,
I giggle, with my senses woke.

Rain might tap like a funny tune,
But I'm the boss—no need to swoon.
With laughter bright, I'm always warm,
In this playful shelter from the storm.

Under the Canopy of Safety

Under leafy greens and a pillow fort,
I host my friends, we never cut short.
Snacks on hand, a feast divine,
With laughter mixing in the wine.

In a secure place only we can see,
A world of nonsense, wild and free.
Like superheroes in a playful spree,
We make great plans while sipping tea.

Pajama parties with goofy style,
Tickle fights ensue, laughter for a while.
With stories spun like sugary yarn,
Under this canopy, we can charm.

So let the outside world be bold,
With playful hearts, we'll never grow old.
Together we giggle, spin, and play,
In our happy haven, night or day.

The Shielding Canopy

Under the branches I scoot,
Dodging splashes from my fruit.
Birds squawk above, quite the chatter,
Still I'm here, no need for the latter.

Raindrops dance like little bees,
Tickling my head with such great ease.
With my hat and a sunny grin,
I laugh as the weather lets me win.

Squirrels plot my downfall's delight,
As they dart left, then take flight.
Chasing shadows, I start to roam,
Beneath this madcap leafy dome.

Nature's joke is quite the jest,
In this hodgepodge, I find my rest.
A shelter built with laughs and cheer,
Who knew protection could come from here?

Trees of Support

Among the trunks, I blend and sway,
As leaves gossip about the day.
"Honey, where's my lunch?" one tree calls,
While squirrels plan their acorn brawls.

Branches reach, all bending low,
As if to catch me like a pro.
Twirling 'neath this leafy crown,
Strutting 'round like I'm the town's clown.

Roots are tangled like my last night,
Trying to stand straight but not quite.
Every rustle's a tickled tease,
In this forest, I'm quite at ease.

The wood whispers jokes above my head,
I can't help but giggle instead.
Together we share this merry spree,
Those trees sure know how to party!

A Refuge from the Noise

When the world buzzes like a swarm,
I seek a place that feels like warm.
No honks or shouts, just a rustling sound,
In my quiet nook, peace is found.

Crickets tickle my eardrums soft,
As I snicker at clouds aloft.
They bumble about, shapes in the sky,
Who knew they had such a funny mind's eye?

From raucous crowds, I gladly flee,
To my cozy den of laughter and glee.
With each tick and tock from the trees,
Nature's giggles put me at ease.

Here, time stops and dances slow,
As breezes tease me to and fro.
In this refuge where silly prevails,
I wave goodbye to life's loud gales.

Echoes of Safety

In the nook where shadows play,
Whispers bloom like flowers in May.
Giggles bounce off every wall,
Here I can laugh without a call.

Echoes dance like they own the space,
Imitating my silly face.
"Who's the goof?" the branches sing,
While I prance and twirl, doing my thing.

The chitter of leaves, a playful tease,
Nature nudges me, "So take it easy!"
As shadows echo, my heart feels light,
In this safe haven, my worries take flight.

With each rustle, I join the spree,
No worries here, just me and glee.
In this space where laughter rings,
I find refuge in tiny things.

Vault of Resilience

When rain drops down like clumsy cats,
I just think of my cozy mats.
My walls are thick, they laugh and sway,
As squirrels hold conferences all day.

The wind may howl a merry tune,
While shadows dance beneath the moon.
I sip my tea and watch the show,
While raccoons play on the window.

A leaky roof? A silly plight!
I name each drip, my day's delight.
With jars on hand like open arms,
I catch the drops, my house's charms.

And when the storms come howling near,
I twirl beneath my umbrella cheer.
This vault of laughter, warm and bright,
Keeps me safe, giggling all night.

Horizon of Protection

In the morning light, I see the fun,
As breakfast meets the morning run.
The toaster sputters, the coffee spills,
A circus act of kitchen thrills.

Pillows pile like clouds of joy,
My dog thinks he's a mighty ploy.
He guards my snacks with a fierce bark,
While birds outside make quite the remark.

My curtains wave like dancers true,
Inviting breezes to join the crew.
The laundry billows, a flag of cheer,
Waving freedom, come join us here!

So here I stand, my heart aglow,
With piles of laughter in steady flow.
This horizon smiles in bright display,
Where every mishap becomes a play.

Stronghold of Peace

Here in my fortress, a snack attack,
I dodge the crumbs that try to track.
A fortress built from soft pillows,
Where giggles echo, and joy follows.

The mailman trips, but oh what fun!
He waves and laughs, a daily run.
While cats on windowsills strike poses,
In this kingdom where humor never dozes.

My vacuum roars like dragons wild,
As I'm chased around, a playful child.
With each fight against dust bunnies,
I declare myself the king of funnies.

And so I dwell, my heart at ease,
Where chaos reigns and laughter's breeze.
In this stronghold of silliness, I thrive,
In a world where smiles stay alive.

Trusting the Skylight

A skylight opens to the grainy sky,
Where birds debate on paths to fly.
They chirp about their lunch spots near,
While I just giggle at their cheer.

Sunbeams filter like golden jam,
As I dance around, a happy sham.
And when it rains, I laugh and grin,
Each drop a drummer, tapping in.

My plants all sway like they're in a band,
Doing their best to make a stand.
They cheer me on as I try to sing,
The skylight's warmth is the real thing!

With every breeze, a tickle plays,
As clouds gather for an impromptu rave.
So here's to the view that brings delight,
Where whimsy sings into the night!

The Embrace of Home

A place where socks mysteriously hide,
And crumbs cuddle along for the ride.
Where laughter echoes in joyous cheer,
And every corner feels oddly near.

In the kitchen, chef chaos unfolds,
Spaghetti on walls, and stories retold.
The dog steals my sandwich, what a delight!
In this quirky palace, all feels just right.

The laundry basket, a mountain of dread,
Socks like orphan puppies, searching for bread.
With every step, I trip on a shoe,
Yet in this circus, my heart's still true.

Under this quirky, unpredictable roof,
Life's little shenanigans bring me my proof.
In a world full of chaos, I dance and I play,
For this merry madness is home every day.

Shield from Shadows

When raindrops tap a rhythm on high,
I grab my umbrella, oh my oh my!
That goofy thing flips, it takes to the sky,
But here in my bubble, I just can't cry.

The cats claim their thrones on my cozy chair,
Leaving fuzz on my clothes, as they lounge without care.
They plot their great heists for the last turkey slice,
But who can resist those feline devices?

With every thunderclap shaking the ground,
I snuggle with blankets, so sweet and round.
The shadows might dance like some eerie ballet,
But I laugh at the jokes that they try to play.

So here's to that shelter from lightning's loud pop,
With my trusty old couch that just won't stop.
In this goofy domain where oddities bloom,
I shield myself from the storm, in my room.

Sanctuary of Stars

Beneath the blanket of twinkling light,
I ponder my snacks, the sweet and the bright.
The fridge hums softly, a nocturnal friend,
As midnight munchies round the curve, they bend.

Pajama-clad wonders roam wild in the night,
Dreams of grandeur as I take flight.
But landing in socks that have gone astray,
Turns my grand adventure to a comical fray.

Here, the ceiling seems to whisper and sigh,
As I talk to the shadows of bees flying by.
Each crumb on my bed tells a tale of delight,
Of midnight excursions into pure dynamite.

In this laughing galaxy, I hum and I sway,
Each star a reminder, it's okay to play.
With dreams in my heart and a giggle or five,
This sanctuary of stars keeps the fun alive.

Safe Haven Above

Upstairs, it's chaos, a playful abode,
Where laundry piles up like a mountain road.
I peek at the bathroom, oh what a sight,
Toothpaste cap wars, they just love to fight!

The t.v. blares music that's stuck in my head,
I'm singing along with the cat on my bed.
He rolls and he purrs, then he knocks over,
My soda can dreams turned fridge takeover!

Here in the nooks are my treasures galore,
Doodles and snacks on the bedroom floor.
My safe haven above, it's a whimsical spree,
Where laughter is crafted from the absurdity.

So here's to the chaos, to triumphs and falls,
To dust bunnies cheering through those empty halls.
In this wonky haven where stories collide,
Life's just more fun with laughter as our guide.

Shelter Beneath the Stars

A house of quirks with creaks and squeaks,
Where every bump is laughter's peaks.
The roof a hat, quite out of place,
It wobbles in the evening's grace.

With shingles peeling like a ripe banana,
A quirky home, a grand nirvana.
I raise my cup to every leak,
The drip-drops harmonize, so to speak.

The squirrels tap dance, a furry show,
While raindrops sing in a rhythmic flow.
Each storm a party, each breeze a cheer,
In this goofy haven, there's naught to fear.

So here's to laughter, in this silly space,
A home where life wears a grin on its face.
No need for caution, just let it be,
In my roof-friend's laughter, I feel so free.

Guardian Overhead

Oh guardian of shingles, stout and bold,
You guard my dreams, both young and old.
With every creak and groan you make,
You're the best comedy show for free's stake.

When rain pitter-patters on the tin,
I chuckle at the thought of my win.
"Dance on, you droplets, get funky there!"
"Let's see who'll steal my sleep if you dare!"

A roof that sings with the wind's sweet tune,
Like a wacky hat on a cartoon.
Each leak a giggle, a splashing joke,
I tap my toes, while my neighbors croak.

With every gust, my spirits lift high,
I chuckle beneath this jokester sky.
So here's to my guardian, old and silly,
In its wobbly shade, I find true glee.

Haven of Dreams

In this quirky nook where giggles thrive,
My rooftop's a party, oh, how it's alive!
With stars peeking in like guests at a door,
Ready to join in, for laughter's core.

, The tiles may shuffle, a cha-cha-cha,
While I dance with shadows, like a superstar.
Each flowerpot jokes, a blooming delight,
In this haven of dreams, everything's bright.

The chimney's a storyteller, puffing out tales,
With puffs of smoke, it never fails.
And spiders web up their feathery threads,
Sewing laughter into all of our beds.

So raise a toast to this funny old place,
Where every corner holds a smiling face.
A riddle of joy, where dreams come to play,
In this haven so wacky, I choose to stay.

Whispering Eaves

The eaves chat softly, gossiping rain,
"Did you hear that one? Oh, what a gain!"
In whispers they tell of the squirrels' delight,
The nutty escapades in the dead of night.

With each gust of wind, a tickle or poke,
A comedy sketch from this rooftop cloak.
"Did you check the gutter? It's all belly laughs!"
Each shingle a joker, with wacky gaffes.

The raindrops a chorus, a fanciful song,
I join the tune when the night gets long.
"Let's dance with the thunder, let's sway with the breeze!"
Together we giggle, with effortless ease.

So here's to the whispers of windy refrain,
In this castle of fun, never mundane.
With laughter above, I'm never alone,
Under this roof, I'm always at home.

Canopy of Dreams

Underneath this shade so wide,
I hide from thoughts I cannot bide.
Sipping tea and napping slow,
While squirrels put on a funny show.

A leaf fell down, did a little dance,
It twirled around like it had a chance.
I chuckled loud, the wind did sigh,
Even nature can laugh, oh my!

Raindrops play a silly tune,
They drum on me like a cartoon.
With this cover, I'm safe and snug,
Hugging my pillow, feeling a hug.

Stars peek through with bright, cheeky grins,
Making wishes where laughter begins.
So here I dwell 'neath this frisky dome,
In my funny world, I'm always home.

Shelter of Serenity

This cozy pad, a happy place,
Where socks do tango, and pillows race.
Chirping birds gossip loud all day,
In this living room, we laugh and play.

The sunlight beams like a quiet clown,
Tickling me softly; I almost frown.
But oh, I giggle, my heart takes flight,
In this peculiar, playful light.

Cats plot mischief on their throne,
While dogs snore loudly, lost in the zone.
Beneath this space, we dance and twirl,
In our bubble of fun, we safely whirl.

With each rustle, a prank unfolds,
Nature's joke is fun and bold.
So here I stay, in laughter's grace,
In my silly shelter, I find my place.

Embrace of Eternity

This grand embrace, it wraps me tight,
With cushions, blankets, pure delight.
Every creak is a giggle grand,
In my wacky fort made by hand.

I'm queen of chaos, ruler of naps,
As the cat's on guard, avoiding mishaps.
Each time a friend pops by for tea,
We share jokes, oh how silly we be!

Cards fly high, laughter bursts,
With every quirk, our joy just thirsts.
In this vast realm of shenanigans bright,
We twirl and leap into the night.

Time drifts gently, like leaves on streams,
Wrapped tight here, we build our dreams.
So let the world outside go round,
In this zany haven, happiness found.

The Topic Above

Oh, the thing that tops a house so right,
Keeps me dry and out of sight.
With shingles dancing in the breeze,
It's the crown for my happy tease.

Pigeons perch with a snarky laugh,
Eyeing my tasty pizza half.
It shields not just from rain and snow,
But from my neighbor's wild banjo show!

Every storm tries to tap-dance here,
But I just chuckle, holding dear.
In this giggle dome, I'm here to stay,
With my friends, we'll always play.

So lift your spirits; let's toast this cap,
To the fun that sparks in our cozy lap.
In this frolic fortress above, we thrive,
With laughter and joy, we feel alive!

Enveloping Peace

Beneath a ceiling so very high,
I wave at pigeons who just fly by.
They tease me with crumbs, oh what a joke,
As I munch on snacks, my laughter awoke.

The walls might shake with every slight quake,
But here I stay, it's my own little lake.
With banana peels and socks on the floor,
This lovely chaos, who could want more?

The sound of rain is a symphony,
It's just my cat, not a ghost, can't you see?
She leaps through the air, a true acrobat,
Under this cover, I just tip my hat.

So here's to this shelter, my quirky retreat,
Where neighbors think twice before they compete.
With laughter and snacks, I sit back and play,
In this jolly haven, I'll happily stay.

Perched in Stillness

In a fort of blankets, I sit and I scheme,
A throne of cushions, a child's wild dream.
The cat looks at me like I'm out of my head,
But I'm just a queen in this fortress of thread.

The light is dim, and I can't see straight,
But snacks are all here; it's truly first-rate.
Laughter erupts with each squishy bite,
In my cozy kingdom, everything's right.

A squirrel passes by, offering a wave,
But I'm too busy plotting, my snacks I must save.
With crumbs on my shirt and a giggle to spare,
I reign over chaos, with dust in my hair.

Oh, to be perched on this throne made of fluff,
The laughter I burst with is more than enough.
Each giggle a note, in this world full of fun,
In my fortress of calm, I'm never outdone.

Fortified by Love

Here in my castle, I'm safe and secure,
With cookies aplenty and hugs that endure.
Mom's secret recipe, they're baked with a grin,
My fortress of sweetness, let the fun begin!

My pup plays sentry, all barking and cheer,
A furry protector, never shows fear.
He guards my last cookie, his eyes all aglow,
In this wacky realm, love's the real show.

Colorful paintings cover the walls,
Each brushstroke whispers, "Come one, come all!"
With laughter we echo, the joy we create,
In this love-fortress, there's never a weight.

So let the wild world rumble and roar,
I've got my pals, what could I ask more?
With whimsy and giggles, I'll run with delight,
In my fortress of laughter, my heart feels so light.

The Skies That Shield

High on my perch, I look up and see,
Clouds parade by, just as silly as me.
A duck flies past, wearing a hat,
Are those feathers or fluff? I can't find a mat!

With peeks of the sun, the warmth hugs me tight,
Like a big, goofy bear, in the day and the night.
I wave at the stars; they twinkle with glee,
In this wacky glow, I'm as free as a bee.

The winds tease my hair, now it's wild and grand,
Like a soft spaghetti, it twists on demand.
Up here in the heights, I practice my dance,
With joy in my heart, I take every chance.

So here's to the skies, with all their grand dreams,
They cradle my laughter, my whimsy, my schemes.
In this loony expanse, I'll forever reside,
With a chuckle on high, where pure joy won't hide.

Shelter from the Tempest

When raindrops dance and play,
I hide beneath my snug display.
A leaky roof, oh what a treat,
It's like a shower on my feet!

Thunder rolls, and I just grin,
My ceiling's got a drip like sin.
With bowls and buckets on the floor,
I call it art and nothing more!

Windy gusts that roam and sway,
Turn my living room to a spray.
The dog looks up, with silly glee,
This stormy life is fun for me!

So let it rain, let tempests blow,
I'll keep on laughing, don't you know?
In puddles, I'll take all my steps,
A flooded room? Just fancy reps!

Refuge in the Night

When darkness wraps its velvet cape,
I snuggle up, my safety tape.
A bed so fine, like fluff and dreams,
I drift away on moonlit beams.

Oh, what a comfort, soft and round,
A pillow fortress, snug and sound.
The shadows dance, but I won't fret,
My midnight snack's the best, you bet!

The clock goes tick, the world is still,
I sneak a snack against my will.
The fridge is glowing, a beacon bright,
A sneaky feast in the dead of night!

So here I lay, in cozy bliss,
A comfy kingdom, hard to miss.
With blankets piled, I take my flight,
In slumber deep, till morning light!

The Umbrella of Home

An umbrella sits by the door,
It's broken, bent, and needs much more.
But when the skies are gray and drear,
   I wield it like a knight, oh dear!

With every drip and drop that falls,
I prance around like I've won balls.
A shield of shade from sun's harsh beam,
   In squishy shoes, I chase the dream!

Neighbors stare as I parade,
A royal fool in joyful raid.
"Look at him, that quirky champ!"
My wet attire, my grand swamp camp!

So let it pour, let breezes blow,
With my fine hat, I'm ready, whoa!
For every storm that comes my way,
   Drenched in laughter, I'll still play!

Above the Worries

High on a roof, I take my stand,
With visions grand across the land.
The squirrels shout, teamed up in jest,
Whilst I just lounge, I'm quite the guest!

With wind in hair and sun-kissed brow,
I wave at clouds; I'll take a bow.
"Come join me up here, friends galore!"
We're planning mischief, who could ask for more?

The pigeons coo, they plot my schemes,
Above it all, I'm lost in dreams.
When life gets tough, I soar above,
The world is funny, just like love!

So here I stay, with laughter loud,
My rooftop stage, I'm feeling proud.
In silliness, I find my peace,
With a wink and grin, my joys increase!

A Fortress of Familiarity

In my cozy nook, I plot and scheme,
Dreaming of pizza and vanilla ice cream.
The walls are my bros, they never complain,
Even when my cat decides to play with the rain.

My ceiling's a shield from the wild squirrel dance,
Who thinks my roof is the stage for romance.
With a gentle thud, they take their best shot,
But my fortress stands strong, laughs off their plot.

Here I can dance in my mismatched socks,
Twirl around thoughts like they're quirky blocks.
Each wall has a joke, each beam tells a tale,
In this hilarious haven, I set my own sail.

So here's to the space where laughter's the key,
My fortress of fun, just my cat and me.
We'll toast to the snacks and the comfort we keep,
In this goofy retreat, I never lose sleep.

The Sky's Beneath My Feet

Under this roof, I take silly leaps,
With dreams that are wacky and joy that creeps.
My head's in the clouds, while my feet dance below,
In a world where rubber chickens put on a show.

The floor's my trampoline, bouncy and bright,
With every wild jump, I'm ready for flight.
Though gravity tugs, I still take my stand,
With a giggle and wiggle, I conquer the land.

Mice peek from corners, in tuxedos they prance,
While I take a moment to join in their dance.
The ceiling's a canvas for thoughts that I sketch,
As giggles erupt like a bubbly good fetch.

So let me embrace this circus of glee,
Where laughter and chaos form harmony.
In this upside-down world, I'm ever so fleet,
With the sky beneath me and silliness sweet.

A Lid on Life's Chaos

I've got a lid on things, or so I declare,
In this wild bustling kitchen, I twirl without care.
Spatulas dancing, a whisk takes a bow,
While dishes conspire to give me a wow.

Here, chaos is cozy, it blends like a stew,
With a sprinkle of chaos and a dash of goo.
The fridge sings a tune, the oven joins in,
As I juggle my snacks like an acrobat's spin.

There's flour in my hair, oh what a delight,
As I strut like a chef in my sweet culinary fight.
With aprons as capes, we save the day,
Battling messes, come what may.

So here's to the mayhem we call a home,
Where laughter's the spice and we freely roam.
In my lid of chaos, I'll never feel lone,
I dance with my dishes, together our zone.

Bound by the Beams

These beams are my buddies, my pals in disguise,
Holding up secrets and practical lies.
They creak in agreement when I tell a dumb joke,
With laughter that echoes, the best kind of folk.

I've tethered my dreams to these sturdy old lines,
Making wishes like kids on a swing set of twines.
Each knot ties a story, each rafter a goal,
In this whimsical web that feeds my soul.

Decorated with memories, these beams know my name,
Whispering softly, "We're all in this game."
Together we thrive in this wonderful space,
Tied up in laughter, we create our own grace.

So let's raise a glass to the humor we bind,
In the structure of chaos where joy isn't blind.
With beams as my anchor and giggles my quest,
I find my true home, where I smile and jest.

Held by the Heavens

Up high there's a shield from the rain,
A big umbrella where birds complain.
While clouds gather, I don't fret,
For my dreams are safe, you bet!

Squirrels dance, they entertain,
Juggling acorns—what a gain!
The wind can howl, but I just laugh,
Because nature's humor is my staff.

A spot for my hat, a shade for my drink,
Here's where I plot and think.
If it falls apart, I'll just wear a grin,
With such a view, how can I lose or win?

So when storms roar and skies go gray,
I choose to play, let the rain spray.
I might get soaked, but that's just fine,
With laughter and joy, I'll brightly shine!

Anchor of Assurance

In this quirky treehouse, oh what a sight,
With walls made of laughter, it feels just right.
The squirrels gossip, the owls debate,
While I sip my cocoa, life's really first-rate.

Neighbors complain that my roof's quite old,
But wisdom comes wrapped in stories told.
A leak here and there? It's part of the charm,
Just a splash of water, who needs alarm?

Cracks in the ceiling? It adds some flair,
As raindrops dance, it's a lively affair.
Flying the flag of 'it's all okay',
I'll brew more coffee, and dance the day away.

So here in my haven, I'm never alone,
With laughter as wallpaper, it feels like home.
Let the wind blow wild and the storms unfurl,
In my anchor of assurance, I'll give them a whirl!

The Safety Net Above

Above me hangs a safety net, so grand,
It's not silk or satin, just fruit from the land.
Bananas and oranges, a fruity surprise,
It catches my worries and flings them to skies.

The birds throw parties; they sing and chirp,
Celebrating life with each little burp.
While I dangle below like a merry clown,
Who needs more chaos when you wear a crown?

You might think it's silly, a net made of cheer,
But every fall's softer than it does appear.
Just giggles and rainbows, with each little crash,
I bounce back up—it's an unbeatable smash!

So high above troubles, I float with delight,
In a world of silliness, everything's right.
Let the world spin wild, and let it all fall,
For I'm wrapped in comfort, the funniest of all!

Cloak of Protection

Snug in my blanket—a cloak made of dreams,
It wraps me in giggles and warm, silly schemes.
While clouds let loose, I stay cozy and tight,
As my superhero, I take on the night.

The wind bears tales of adventures untold,
Encounters with dragons, it's pure comic gold.
With every gust, I just shake my head,
And wrap tighter in laughter, no fear, just spread!

Raindrops may patter, but they don't stand a chance,
My cloak of protection is all in the dance.
So let the storms rumble and thunder come down,
I'm safe here, indulging, wearing my crown.

Each giggle a raindrop, each snicker a shield,
In this silly fortress, I'll never yield.
With humor my armor, I stand here today,
Cloaked in giggles, come what may!

Vaulting the Threats

When rain starts to dance on my hat,
I smile and enjoy the splat.
A puddle forms right beneath my feet,
Splish-splashing feels like a treat.

The sun peeks through clouds with glee,
Sunglasses on, looking fancy-free.
I dodge a bird, oh dodging with flair,
As it aims for my snack with great care.

Wind howls like a jester in play,
Tugging my coat in a funny way.
A tumbleweed rolls down the street,
It gives me a challenge, oh what a feat!

With friends nearby, we laugh and boast,
Chasing the squirrels, toast to our host!
In this chaos of weather's parade,
My joy can't fade, it's home that I've made.

The Shelter Above

A ceiling so high, it casts a wide net,
Down comes a bird, oh what a pet!
Tap dancing on shingles, it makes quite a show,
As I sit with my popcorn, ready for the flow.

Pigeons wear suits, looking so grand,
Fluffing their feathers, they form a band.
Their songs are a mixture of honks and coos,
Who knew my roof had such wacky views?

When storms come crashing, I stay warm and dry,
And pigeons at play just lift my spirits high.
I join the chaos with a laugh and a cheer,
In this quirky abode, I have nothing to fear.

A slice of pizza from the neighbor's stash,
We feast on the roof, watching the splashes.
With every weird moment, my heart starts to swell,
In this abode of fun, all is well.

Beneath the Guardian Wings

Beneath a sky that sings with flair,
I dance like no one else is there.
The clouds above are fluffy like cake,
I giggle as the raindrops make me shake.

Squirrels perform acrobatics in the trees,
Their antics tickle me, like a gentle breeze.
A wise old crow gives me a wink,
'Just don't step on those ants!' he says with a blink.

With each gust of wind, I hold on tight,
But the patio table is my knight in white.
Playing hide and seek from the drops above,
In this silly game, I've found my love.

The moon joins the party, winking down low,
Sharing laughs with stars, putting on a show.
In this embrace, I feel so light,
Beneath my guardian wings, everything's bright.

A Doorway to Rest

I open my door to a world of surprise,
Where socks become gremlins and dance in the skies.
A chair shouts, 'Sit, take a load off!',
While my cat gives me sass with a cough.

The fridge hums a tune like a radio star,
Beaming with snacks and a bright candy jar.
I gather a feast for a grand little bite,
Each chip in my bowl aims for greatness tonight.

A pillow fight breaks with a swing and a shove,
Laughter erupts, oh such pure love.
The walls crack a joke, laughter without end,
In this door to fun, I find my best friend.

As bedtime approaches, the giggles still flow,
In this cozy hideaway, I'm ready to glow.
With dreams of socks and dancing cats,
I drift into slumber, cozy with laughs.

Under the Gaze of the Moon

Oh how I dance in the bright moonlight,
The cat laughs at my silly sight.
With shadows prancing, I spin around,
Crickets chirping, the only sound.

The stars wink down with a giggle or two,
As I trip over my shoelace, oh what a view!
Jumping puddles that I can't see,
The night is young, and so am I, whee!

Security Beneath the Shingles

Under shingles, my worries take flight,
The squirrels plot mischief by day and by night.
I stash snacks for them, avoiding the mess,
They scurry away, what a lucky guess!

The rain patters down like a playful tune,
While I sip cocoa, singing to the moon.
Mockingbird joins in, that talented fool,
Together we laugh, forgetting the rules.

Enclosure of Tender Thoughts

Here in my nook, cozy as can be,
Dreams float around like a bumblebee.
With pillows stacked high for a soft little throne,
I plot my escape to the unknown.

The curtain flutters, a playful tease,
While I giggle out loud, swaying in the breeze.
Daydreaming boldly, with socks mismatched,
In this sanctuary, joy is hatched.

The Hearth's Guardian

By the crackling fire, I roast marshmallows,
The flames dance wild, like silly fellows.
As I juggle logs with a comical grace,
A spark leaps forth, oh, what a chase!

Resting my chin on the mantelpiece, true,
I hear the stories of old, one or two.
The ghosts in the chimneys chuckle aloud,
In this warm embrace, I'm humorously proud.

Where Shadow Meets Light

Under the sky, I look up high,
Wondering if birds ever get shy.
They flit about, with such a cheer,
While I dodge raindrops, oh dear, oh dear!

With a cap that's crooked, I strut with pride,
Like a funky penguin, I take a slide.
The sun beams down, it's quite a sight,
Making me dance, what a silly plight!

The Shielded Horizon

Beneath the clouds, I roast like a pig,
Yet I'm cool as a cucumber, doing a jig.
A sudden gust knocks me off my feet,
I tumble and roll, quite the fun treat!

Socks on my hands, what a strange sight,
It's a fashion statement, if you get it right.
Chasing my hat as it flies away,
Laughter erupts, on this quirky day!

Cradle of Contentment

In my backyard, the bees buzz by,
Wearing a hat made of pie, oh my!
A picnic spread, just for me and my bread,
To munch on while dreaming instead.

Sipping lemonade, I spill on my shoe,
Laughing at the ruckus in my little zoo.
With squirrels that chatter and dance like fools,
I'm the king of my castle, breaking all rules!

A Canopy of Solace

Beneath the leaves, I take a peek,
Wondering if worms ever feel weak.
They squirm and squiggle, oh so bold,
While I sip my drink, feeling quite old.

A squirrel with style, stealing a snack,
I applaud the mischief, no reason to quack.
In the sunshine's glow, we all come alive,
It's a circus of joy, as we wiggle and jive!

A Crown of Warmth

Above my head, a funny hat,
It keeps me safe, imagine that!
A cozy dome, with jokes inside,
It makes me laugh, like joy's a ride.

When it rains, the jokes drop down,
Splashing giggles all around.
A merry shield from stormy fate,
It serves me snacks while I just wait.

Beneath it all, I dance and sing,
No need for clouds, I'm the king!
With every shade from bright to dark,
This funny crown is quite a spark.

So here I sit, with giggles bold,
Wrapped in warmth, or so I'm told.
This whimsical hat, it makes me sway,
Forever fun, my sunny play.

Beneath the Guardian Sky

Underneath this fluffy dome,
I chuckle softly, far from home.
A guardian sky, with colors bright,
It makes my worries take to flight.

When thunder grumbles, I just grin,
I know the jokes are about to begin.
Like a clownfish in a sea of cheer,
We frolic far away from fear.

The stars above are winking wide,
Nudging me to take a ride.
So here I lay, with dreams in tow,
This silly sky puts on a show.

With every cloud that drifts along,
It whispers secrets, sings a song.
Beneath this dome, I feel alive,
A joyful heart, where laughter thrives.

Wings of Comfort

I've got feathers, bright and neat,
They flap around like dancing feet.
These wings of comfort, so light and free,
They tickle my sides, oh joyfully!

When the wind whispers silly tales,
And laughter swirls like fishy scales.
I float above the mundane ground,
With jokes on wings, I spin around.

In this cozy nest, I take a dive,
The giggles bring me much alive.
With every flap, I soar in glee,
A feathered friend, that's truly me!

So when you call, just look up high,
You'll see my wings against the sky.
Together in fun, we'll take our flight,
With laughter's wind, we'll dance all night!

A Covering of Hope

Beneath this blanket of dreams and cheer,
Laughter snuggles up right near.
A quirky quilt, all patched and bright,
It warms my soul, both day and night.

When twilight falls, I pull it tight,
This covering of hope feels just right.
Jokes woven in, like playful threads,
Wrap me up snug, along with my beds.

If storms should come, I simply grin,
For I know that fun is where I've been.
In cracks of light, the gags will shine,
With every squeak, the giggles align.

So take a chance, toss cares away,
Join my quilt and laugh all day.
With warmth so grand and spirits bright,
Together we bask in pure delight.

Barriers Against the Gales

When the wind starts to howl, I just laugh,
My umbrella's my shield, when it's half a giraffe.
The squirrels mock my fashion, it's quite the sight,
But I twirl like a dancer, my spirits take flight.

Neighbors peek through curtains, with cups and with fear,
Watching me wobble, then laugh, shed a tear.
A gust lifts my hat, oh what a bold scene,
Twirling like crazy, like I'm living a dream.

There's humor in nature, you just have to see,
A raised voice of thunder can't bother me!
I'll prance in the puddles, make splashes and swirls,
Life's too short to hide, I'd rather do twirls.

So here's to the storms, and the winds that may shout,
I'll dance through the rain, and I won't have a doubt.
Each gale is a challenge, a laugh in the rain,
With a heart filled with joy, I'll charm the mundane.

The Ceiling of Care

Under this peculiar, wobbly frame,
A place full of laughter, but never the same.
I've got pizza on Fridays and socks without pairs,
The ceiling is low, but the joy fills the airs.

Mom says it's cozy, but I just can't agree,
How can I grow when I'm stuck to my knee?
When it rains, I just grin, it's a wild, fun ride,
Dodge drops like they're dodgeballs, with friends by my side.

The roof creaks a bit, like a hearty old friend,
Told me to settle, but I just can't pretend.
The ceiling may limit, but my spirit can soar,
With giggles and snacks, who could ask for more?

In this house of quirks, adventures unfold,
Each day a new tale, more funny than bold.
So let the rain pour, let the thunder be proud,
In my ceiling of care, I'll laugh (very loud!).

Canopy of Compassion

Beneath this odd canvas, my life's like a show,
With clowns and with tears and a pie in the dough.
The laughter it echoes, the silliness reigns,
In this canopy shelter, where joy breaks the chains.

The cat's on the table, the dog wears my hat,
In a world full of chaos, can you imagine that?
I trip on the carpet, then leap with great flair,
This canopy's magic can lighten the air.

When friends drop by quickly, it's always a feast,\nThey tumble on couches, a ruckus released.
A dance in the living room, we boogie and wiggle,
Who needs a dance floor when you've got a big giggle?

So we toast to the mishaps, the silly, the fun,
In the shade of this haven, we shine like the sun.
Compassion's the laughter, the love we all share,
In this canopy world, we find joy everywhere.

Quiet Retreat from Chaos

In my tiny flat, where socks go to hide,
The chaos is cozy, so I take it in stride.
With mismatched furniture, it's quiet (unheard),
A retreat from the whirlwind, as funny as blurred.

Jellybeans scatter, a trail to my chair,
Where I sip on my soda, without a single care.
The clock on the wall seems to giggle in time,
While I munch on popcorn, in this chaos sublime.

Neighbors are bustling, with life at full swing,
But here in my bubble, I'm queen of the fling.
A dance with the dust bunnies, they shimmy around,
In this haven I've claimed, life's joys can be found.

So when chaos knocks, I just open the door,
And invite it to step in, while I roll on the floor.
For in this quiet chaos, I'm blushing with cheer,
In my strange little refuge, each day's a wild year.

The Arch of Safety

In my quirky fortress, I dance and sing,
Where cats wear hats and the doorbell's a ring.
Umbrellas are swords in this soft, silly space,
I giggle at raindrops, they can't keep the pace.

Socks on the ceiling, a sight to behold,
The furniture whispers the secrets of old.
With a sandwich for armor, I'm ready to sway,
In this comical kingdom, I swing all day.

Above the World

Upstairs in my castle, the clouds come to play,
With bubbles for chairs in a whimsical way.
The coffee pot laughs as it brews with a grin,
While my reflection teaches the dance of a spin.

When the sun throws a party and moon crashes late,
I swing from the ceiling, I dance on my plate.
The walls wear confetti, a colorful skin,
As I start the giggles that bubble within.

Below the Sky

In my fortress below, the sky looks so bright,
With pizza for ceilings, oh what a delight!
The chairs tell bad jokes as I sip lemonade,
I tickle the curtains in my playful parade.

On Wednesdays, we wear armor of sponge and of cheese,

With sneezes for thunder, and laughter, a breeze.
Dancing with shadows, I'll waltz through the room,
Where each little giggle ignites like a bloom.

A Safe Nest

In my cozy coop, I nestle each day,
Where the fridge plays the trumpet and sings in ballet.
Waffles are warriors that take up the fight,
As I twirl through the kitchen, a jubilant sight.

The spoons hold a dance-off, the toaster gives cheer,
While the cabinets nod along, making it clear.
In this savory hangout, I'm king of my rest,
With pancakes for armor, I feel truly blessed.

Serenity in the Attic

In my attic retreat, where the shadows are bright,
The dust bunnies giggle, a laugh in the night.
With a hammock for dreams and a fan for the breeze,
I nap on a cloud of fluffy cotton cheese.

The mothballs recite tales of adventures so grand,
While the lightbulb whispers secrets I've planned.
In this topsy-turvy, hilarious lair,
I concoct all my dreams with utmost flair!

www.ingramcontent.com/pod-product-compliance
Lightning Source LLC
Chambersburg PA
CBHW050307120526
44590CB00016B/2529